A Degree of Verse
by
Margaret Marsh

This book is dedicated to
all who have inspired, encouraged,
enraged and amused me.

Grosvenor Graphics

Published works include poems in:
Verses of Love ~ Arrival Press Ltd
Paws for Thought ~ Arrival Press Ltd
Just the Tonic ~ Arrival Press Ltd

and
The Blue Line ~ Grosvenor Graphics

Copyright © Margaret Marsh 2000

All rights reserved. No part of this publication may be reproduced, stored in a retrieval system, or transmitted in any form or by any means, electronic, mechanical, photocopying, recording or otherwise, without the prior permission of the publisher.

ISBN 0-9538655-0-9

Published by
Grosvenor Graphics
7 Bank House Lane ~ Helsby ~ Cheshire ~ WA6 0PS

FOREWORD

My family is grown up now, with Degrees, all three.
My husband got his years ago, so that left only me.
I sent for the brochure, thinking "I'll do one myself,
At Open University, then I'm not left on the shelf."

But as I looked at the courses and the time required,
I realised that just reading it left me very tired.
So, one night in the pub, a solution was found,
I'd write lots more poems and then have them bound.

I started writing poetry when I was only ten.
I only can remember one from way back then.
I wrote a little Limerick for all in Class 1A.
I really do regret having thrown them all away.

I have had several published in more recent years,
Bullied into 'submission' by my two loving dears.
My daughters made me do it, so they're the ones to blame.
They told me I could do it and rekindled that old flame.

My poetry's very personal, it all comes from my heart.
But people that I know and love, all have played their part.
Friends and loved ones, even the dog has not been spared.
But if you've got a mention at least you know I cared.

I don't follow any pattern, I wait until it flows.
I write it as it comes to me, not in 'sonnet' or in prose.
My only qualifications are as mother and as wife
But this is <u>my</u> degree, from the University of Life.

Written about Ken Shepherd in Class 1A
Goole Grammar School
1956

There was a young boy called Shepherd,
Who liked his potatoes peppered.
He made them so hot,
He got up like a shot.
That poor young boy called Shepperd

CONTENTS

My Dream Man	1
One Day to Go	2
The Black Hole	3
I'm Not Bothered	4
The Rat Race	5
Dear Customers	6
The Innocence of a 2-year Old	7
The Diary of Me	8

A Collection of Birthday Celebrations

Happy Birthday, Rob	9
To Sarah, Happy Birthday	10
Happy Birthday, Anne-Louise	11
An Ode to Nora	12/13
Olivia - Happy 18th	14
Happy Birthday, Rick	15
Bryan's Birthday Bash	16
Olga's Birthday Ode	17
Happy Birthday, Kevin	18
Denis, It's Your Birthday	19/20
Up, Up and Away	21/22

The Change	23
Aching (Ageing) Joints	24
My Own Valentine	25
The Alternative Valentine's Ode	26
Mr Chairman, Ladies & Gents	27/29
Lego ~ Boring? ~ Never!	30

CONTENTS continued

Stressful Sunday	31
Battle of the Beef	32/33
Lunch with Lyne	34
Football Fanatic	35
The Blue Line	36/45
The Ladies of M-5-3	45
Thanks to the Pocket Rocket	46
A Special Day	47
Amazing Miss Jones	48
The Ballading Butcher	49

A Few that have been 'Commissioned'

Marriage Lines	50
The Dog House	51
Merry Christmas Sir	52
Engaging Words	53
Moving Times	54
The Doctor's Waiting Room	55/56

Education's a Wonderful Thing

Exam Nerves	57
The Joys of Teaching?	58
James' First	59
Blair's Baby	60
Christmas in Verse	61/62
Summers, Past and Present	63
The Day I Died	64
Slimmers' Plea	65

CONTENTS

To Absent Friends and Loved Ones
My Dad   66/68
To My Mum   69/70
To the Queen of Hearts   71/73
Farewell to Nora   74
One of a Kind   75
The Thief called Death   76
The Thief called Death Revisits   77

A Bundle of Joy, Your Baby Boy   78
Georgio - The Guide   79
Colin's Bottle   80
Get Well Soon   81
Progress ~ A Wondrous Thing?   82
An Insomniac's Dream   83
Nightmare   84
Market Day Madness   85
The Screaming Trees   86
Eleven O'clock - 1 Across   87
Midsummer Madness   88

MY DREAM MAN
Published in 'Verses of Love'.
This is the one that started it all off again

Sorry, no work - my mind is blank.
It's like the weather - dismal and dank.
I need a break from man and kids,
To lie on a beach and close my lids.

A 'Joey Boswell' is what I really need,
A super fellow who will wine and feed,
Hold my hand as I rise from my chair,
Dry my back and kiss under my hair.

I used to have a fellow - just like that.
A man that never left me feeling rather flat.
I lived on laughter, surrounded by love,
Oh, where has he gone? Oh, heavens above....

I know where he is - that man of my dream,
He's the one that annoys me and makes me scream!
Good God - he's my husband, that man of mine,
And I still love him - well, most of the time!

Time and work have shattered the dream,
But we are still friends, a loving team.
One day we'll have time for one another,
Myself and my friend - husband and lover.

ONE DAY TO GO
Published in "Paws for Thought"

I remember the day we went to 'The Pound'
To see all the dogs that had been 'lost' or 'found'.
Hundreds in cages, a terrible sight,
Pets no longer wanted, eyes still bright.

We looked at them all, with tears in our eyes.
It was awful to hear all the pitiful cries.
And then we went to look at 'Death Row',
These poor dogs had maybe only one day to go!

My daughters and I didn't know which to choose,
One would get freedom, the others would lose.
And then we saw him, all dejected and sad,
Sat in the corner as though he'd been bad.

We looked at his face, his eyes now alert,
His head slightly tilted, looking quite pert.
It was love at first sight for Toffee and I.
The girls said, "That's it, we can't let <u>him</u> die."

The door was opened and Toffee was free,
He raced out of that place with positive glee,
Leaped into my car, giving the girls a 'kiss'.
The Pound was a place he wouldn't miss.

He's changed our lives - he's now the boss.
He brightens our days, he never gets cross -
Well, not as long as he gets his way,
Whether it's 'football', 'walk' or simply 'play'!

His hints are subtle - nose to the door,
Or plays 'Sad Sam' with his chin on the floor.
Our lives have been brightened by Toffee, our pet.
A better friend would be so hard to get.

THE BLACK HOLE
Written Wednesday 30th July 1997 at coffee-time!

Our house has a black hole, of that I am quite sure.
It's something I can't fathom and, therefore, cannot cure.
It is the only answer to all the many missing things,
Like socks, pens, money, hankies and my rings.

I can search for a missing object for many, many hours.
It really is amazing how many things the hole devours.
Teaspoons are one of its favourite things to take,
Even the one I've just got out, my coffee about to make.

I turned my back to answer the 'phone, it only took a mo',
And then the spoon had gone and I didn't see it go.
I used to accuse my children of playing a silly prank,
But now we know, it is the hole that we have to thank.

And as for pens and pencils, it drives us all quite mad.
We come to write a little note, a message on the pad,
We have a tub, right by the 'phone, to keep the pens at hand,
But they all seem to vanish, as if it has it planned.

And socks, well they just seem to vanish, I know not where.
I get them ready for the wash and I am sure there is a pair.
I go to hang them on the line and find there's only one...
But now I do not worry 'cos I know just where they've gone!

I'M NOT BOTHERED
Could have been written any shopping day

Why when I ask the question is the reply never true?
Why, if I ask what they want to eat, they haven't got a clue?
Why, if I ask four people, is the answer never the same?
Are they being awkward or is it just a game?

"Don't know" or "I'm not bothered" are regular replies.
They just don't stop to think, when they hear my many sighs.
"SpagBol", "Curry", "Fish'n'chips" or "Pizza" can be heard.
And all I want is to hear them say all the self same word.

I often go out brain-dead and stand in shops, eyes glazed.
Sometimes I seem to get it right, and then I am amazed.
These are educated grown-ups, not thick and not dim-witted.
It's just their brains seem to have certain things omitted.

Like how to make decisions about what they want for tea.
Why does the responsibility always rest with me?
If someone made a product called "Not Bothered" in a tin,
I'd never ever be stuck again, I'd always have some in!

THE RAT RACE
Written one day that had gone 'pear-shaped'

Life seems so full of worry and stress,
Some days at work I feel under duress.
The pace is so fast and no-one has time.
The quality is missing, ain't it a crime?

Where are the days when everyone cared,
When laughter and happiness were what we shared?
Now it's the hustle and bustle, the race is on.
Chasing a living, but your sanity has gone.

Most working folk are feeling depressed,
Their real personalities are being suppressed.
We're becoming like robots, working all day.
Well sod it! I quit! I want to PLAY!

DEAR CUSTOMERS
Yet another frustrating day in the office

"Can I have these done quickly - tomorrow will do?"
Don't these folk realise they're joining a queue?
Why is it always a last minute panic?
Don't they realise they're driving me manic?

I can work very hard but try as I may
I never get more than 24 hours per day.
They ring me at tea-time or late at night.
No matter what time, they feel they've the right.

I try to please everyone, but can't always cope,
The deadlines are kept ~ well that's what I hope.
I only wish that these people could see
That Grosvenor Graphics is me, and just ME!

THE INNOCENCE OF A TWO-YEAR OLD
Written Wednesday before Easter 1998

Imagine the picture, if you can, a queue at a busy check-out.
Couple with children, starting to fratch, Mum is ready to shout.
Dad suggests they look at Easter Eggs, just to keep them quiet,
And off they go, Dad plus four, trying to stop a riot.

The queue is getting longer, someone's paying by cheque.
Then they ask a query, more time wasted ~ oh, heck!
We all stand there, getting cross, tea-time is looming fast.
Our tempers are getting shorter, the mood is overcast.

Just as the queue starts to move, the eldest girl comes back.
She says she likes all the eggs ~ each one in the six foot stack.
Next comes younger sister, full of the joys of Spring.
She's seen a massive one, with chocolates round in a ring.

Then comes the boy, and he's seen one he really likes,
It's a macho one by Cadbury's, especially made for tikes.
And there comes Dad with tot in tow, holding tight her hand,
And we can see, by her face, her speech is ready planned.

She says "Excuse me", so polite, and goes to stand by Mum,
Dad remains where he is and he's looking a little glum.
Mum then asks her youngest child if she has picked an egg.
The answer comes quite slowly, as she hops from leg to leg.

We all stand in silence waiting for the answer, queue forgotten.
We're being rather nosy, listening in, isn't it really rotten?
But then the answer comes and all our moods are changed,
We all wear smiles from ear to ear, looking quite deranged.

"I like the big one in the cupboard at the top of our stairs!"

THE DIARY OF ME - AGE 49 AND A HALF
Published in "Just the Tonic"

Next year it's the BIG ONE, I'll be 'over the hill'...
Well, so they say....but I'm damned if I will!
I can't accept that I'm past my 'sell-by-date',
I had to do something before it's too late.
I've been a rebel for most of my life,
I've never been the mousey housewife.
So I've been and bought my delight of delights...
It's black, it's sporty and it's got pop-up lights!

~~~~~~~~~~~~~~~~~~~~

THE DIARY OF ME - AGE 50 AND A FEW DAYS

Well, I made it to fifty and it's no great big deal,
I find it funny when asked, "So, how does it feel?"
I had a super birthday, flown across the sea,
To play the Casino and the 'chips' were free!
I went to Laxey and saw the wheel from the top
And played 'bandits', Roulette and Blackjack, non-stop.

So I made Five-O without too much fuss,
And, yes I admit, I couldn't run for a bus;
But after a heart-op and battle against big 'C',
It's great to be fifty and I enjoy being ME.
Age is a state of mind and I'm glad to be alive,
And I think I'll grow up when I reach sixty-five!

A COLLECTION OF BIRTHDAY CELEBRATIONS

HAPPY BIRTHDAY, ROB

Written for 7.8.98 having searched in vain for a card with 'Son', nice picture and not too sloppy verse. At the time he was being gazumped on houses with prices like telephone numbers.

Life is full of ups and downs and never more than now,
But Birthdays come to cheer you, so go and show 'em how!
Never mind about tomorrow, today's the one that counts.
So have a super day, Son, forget those house amounts!

TO SARAH
Written for 14th September 1999

I remember the day that you were born,
                twenty-six years today,
You 'walked' out without much fuss,
                "A little girl" I heard them say.
They rushed you to the unit,
                I didn't see you for quite a time.
And then I couldn't hold you
                and tell you that you were mine.

Now you are all grown up,
                you've blossomed through the years.
You're full of love and caring
                with ever-patient listening ears
I'll toast your Birthday later, love,
                whether it's in wine or in water.
To you, Sarah Elizabeth,
                my darling fair-haired daughter

TO ANNE-LOUISE
Written for 14th September 1999

I remember the day that you were born,
                twenty-six years ago,
Born so very tiny, you could have died,
                how I worried so.
You fought for life so fervently,
                usually with a scream.
[It could have come from Stephen King,
                it certainly was no dream]

And now you are a grown up,
                well maybe not so tall,
The schoolkids know you mean it
                when you begin to bawl.
I'll toast your Birthday later, love,
                whether it's in wine or in water.
To you, Anne-Louise, my darling
                dark-haired daughter.

AN ODE TO NORA
Written for my husband, Mike, to read at his Mother's 80th Birthday Party ~ November 1995

A poem to you, Nora, grandma, mother and wife,
Some tales of a woman I've known all of my life.
It started back in Dewsbury, in Nineteen Fifteen,
A Jackson baby girl born with eyes of green.

Growing up between the wars was very very hard,
But you met a young man who was a bit of a card.
Off you would go on your long cycle rides ~
Scarborough and back in the space of three tides!

There's lots of tales of things that you did,
Like the romantic punt on the river Nidd;
A lovely day, at peace in heart and soul,
Then your young beau is stuck up the pole!

Moving to Runcorn, married then with kids,
To pass your driving test you had many bids.
Every Wednesday, to Warrington, with hope,
Then you would come back, all sad, saying "Nope".

But one time, the seventh, you passed the Test,
You're allowed to drive smoothly along with the rest.
You're driving in Liverpool, fast as you like,
When you get overtaken by Plod, on his bike!

A few years on and we're at "Owls Nest",
And a mother's love is put to the test.
I came home drunk and nearly passed out,
"Oh, not my Michael", I heard you shout.

Then Janet is off, going to Canada to stay,
"Don't lose anything", you are heard to say.
You didn't mean 'handbag', we know what you meant.
It was a mother's love with the best intent.

Meat and potato pies, potato cakes too,
These are the foods that remind me of you.
The 'Stand Pies' from Dewsbury, they come still;
And, of course, the POBS when anyone's ill.

Now we are grown up, with children too
And this generation have fond memories of you.
Richard and Andrew, Olivia and Ben,
You'll never be short of a "Few Good Men".

And so we come to this party today,
Your 80th Birthday and I'd just like to say,
On behalf of us all, from far and near ~
Congratulations, Best Wishes and Twenty More Year!

OLIVIA - HAPPY 18th
Written February 1996

Now you're Eighteen, you've got 'The Key',
Quite what to really baffles me!
You've already got one for 'Summerlease',
One for the ignition to go where you please.
To James' heart, you've had that a while,
I guess you got that with a winning smile!

Your family and friends are here today
To share your very special Birthday.
We are here to wish you all the very best,
Viel Glück, Bon Chance and all the rest.
To you, Olivia Ann Louisa Searle,
Congratulations to a special girl.

HAPPY BIRTHDAY, RICK
Written 8th August 1999

On your Birthday you can make a wish
For a VW Beetle or a ten pound fish.
Enjoy your day, just do as you will,
You decide what will fit the bill.
Lazing may be your choice of heaven.
<u>You</u> choose, you're old enough at 27.

BRYAN'S BIRTHDAY BASH
Written in reply to an invitation to
Bryan's Birthday Party on November 20th 1999

Thanks for the invite to Bryan's Party.
We hope he'll be feeling hale and hearty.
We'll come along to make him smile
We haven't seen you for quite a while.

We thought, "He must be 60". We were wrong.
It isn't yet time for <u>that</u> Birthday song!
So this year we'll come and stand in line
To wish you, Bryan, "Happy Fifty Nine".

OLGA'S BIRTHDAY ODE
Written 5th August 1999

"Celebrate in style" is what we say.
Today's your Birthday, <u>your</u> special day.
Forget the housework, no need to cook,
Just have a cuppa and read a book.
We'll drink a toast, in the pub tonight,
Enjoy your meal - don't get too tight!
As another year 'bites the dust' today,
"Celebrate in style" is what we say.

HAPPY BIRTHDAY, KEVIN
Written for the joiner, working here on his birthday

We don't know what you have written
        on your 'wanted' pressie list.
But we hope you have a good day
        and don't get over pissed!
We hope you got a new tape
        'cos the one you've got's quite bent..
We suppose it's just the sort of thing
        your Dad might have sent.

DENIS, IT'S YOUR BIRTHDAY
Written to celebrate his 65th Birthday and Retirement

Here's a Birthday Ode to our friend called Denis,
Known fondly to us as a DIY Menace.
As the 'mover and shaker' of the Manweb empire,
He was the man at the top, a man to admire;
But for us, in the know, he's a walking disaster,
With Anne close behind him, ready with plaster!

Each Sunday morning, in Hunters' Hill,
Out came the mixer, the saw and the drill.
No ordinary mixer, but a big noisy brute,
An industrial model, diesel engine not mute!
Don Lomas would look across the road and say,
"Wonder what the Farquhar boys are doing today?"

Of course, there's the job for Carole and Ceri,
'Twas a bit of a barter, kept everyone merry.
"Leave the mains on, I know what I'm doing."
They should have known that trouble was brewing!
Sparks, they flew from the screwdriver, so bright -
His will had been signed just the previous night!

Then, up at Dave Johnson's, in Dark Lane,
Calamity came Denis's way once again.
He went down the ladder, with tools in hand,
Lost his balance but on the floor did not land.
He clung to the wall and called out for John,
Who stood on his fingers, kept him hanging on!

continued.......

Then there's the tales involving the KCA,
How he put his foot through the ceiling one day.
And another, while planing some wood for the men,
He took off the tops of his fingers, five not ten.
So each time we visit the place for a 'Do',
He remembers the spot where his foot came through.

But one of the best was a classic to boot,
Each time we recall it we just laugh and hoot.
There he was, in thought, in the loo,
When his slow moving car came into view -
With handbrake off, it felled the 'barrow,
Then into Anne's car, straight as an arrow!

One day, last year, he had a nasty fall,
From roof extension he came, tools and all.
He landed, quite hard, on the ground with a splat,
But his life was spared by his tummy fat!
The bruises he showed were blue, green and yellow.
Denis, you really are a very lucky fellow.

Your safest 'stunt' was at the Faraday lecture,
When you 'flew' over New York architecture.
To us, your friends, you're our superman,
You enjoy life to the full, though it worries Anne.
But, joking apart, we wish you Good Health ~
With all those shares, you've got the Wealth!

UP, UP AND AWAY
Written after my Birthday Surprise - October 1995

My Birthday fell on a Saturday this particular year,
My husband said "I have a surprise for you, my dear".
I was told "Don't dress up too smart, jeans will do.
They will be quite OK for where I am taking you."

Off we set, about eleven, heading for North Wales,
The weather is fine with no sign of the forecast gales.
We drive along, going past Sealand and Queensferry.
I love surprises, I'm not concerned, I'm feeling very merry.

As we get our speed up, my curiosity starts to grow,
"Where is it we are going? I'd rather like to know."
Mike says "Look in the glove box, take the paper out.
Do you fancy doing that?" I said "Without a doubt!"

Within a hundred yards, we turned into the site,
My excitement level rose, with not a trace of fright.
I signed the insurance waiver and waited for my go.
The queue was not enormous but it moved on rather slow.

I watched the other people as they went off, then returned.
They all said it was amazing, the adrenalin fair burned!
And then I am at the front, the next one to go is ME,
That's when I thought I was going wobbly at the knee.

Then I'm in the glider, strapped up like a frozen chicken.
Mike is taking pictures, I can hear the camera clicking.
The pilot says "There's no thermals, we won't get long to fly.
But if you want a thrill, then 'loop the loop' we'll try."

continued.....

Off we go, towed along and then we're off the ground.
Then we're soaring, like the birds, not making any sound.
I can see Great Orme, Llandudno, and out across the sea.
Now we're climbing, next we swoop, "Oh, goodness gracious me!"

Now we're up and over, the horizon's upside down,
So's my stomach and my face, gravity makes me frown.
And then we are the right way up, soaring o'er the trees.
"Coming in to land, hands on shoulders, brace your knees."

Safely down at the top of the field, my stomach is still achurn,
But the trip was quite amazing and now Mike'll have his turn.
My Birthday treat was a real surprise, it really was so great.
I feel so lucky that I have got such an imaginative mate.

THE CHANGE
Written on a 'fight with a feather' day, January 1998

What is this thing they call "The Change",
    That affects every woman on earth?
It seems to be such a mystery,
    More than the miracle of Birth.
It brings hot flushes and mood swings.
    Some women could 'fight with a feather'.
And no-one can advise when this will happen,
    It is easier to predict the weather.
Some women claim that they couldn't tell,
    When everything 'started to stop'.
They merely noticed, quite by chance,
    They had stopped their 'monthly' shop.
Now, some women get through it easy,
    And some need some HRT.
But whether it is long or really quite brief
    It is a medical mystery.
And just when you think it's all over
    It catches you quite unaware.
That makes you cross, 'cos it spoils the plan
    Of what you had planned to wear.
You would rather die in a corner,
    Oh, please just leave me alone.
No, I don't want tea and sympathy,
    I'm like a dog worrying a bone!
If men had to tackle the symptoms,
    With all this uncertainty,
They'd soon throw in the towel
    And take to their beds, you'd see.
So how do I get through it all?
    With a man I would gladly exchange.
Swap places for as long as is needed
    To get through this thing called "The Change"

ACHING (AGEING) JOINTS
Written 19th October 1997, the day after a Wedding Reception

In a few more days, I've another one due,
And I admit I'm feeling more 'old' than 'new'.
My mind is quite willing, but the energy's gone.
But then again, on Tuesday I'll be Fifty-One.

I haven't got too many things done today,
A bit of ironing and brushed some leaves away.
A crossword puzzle, then cooked Sunday Dinner.
Now I've eaten it and sloth is the winner.

I think I'll just sit and watch a bit of TV,
Palin then Schindler, for an hour or three!
Is this idle-itis or old age in sight?
No - it's because I was 'Twisting' all last night!

MY OWN VALENTINE
Written after a fruitless search for a suitable card
Valentine's Day, 1999

I searched the shops for hours and hours,
Flicked past bows and hearts and flowers.
Searching for a really special verse...
They seemed to go from bad to worse.

I wanted one that would truly cover
How I feel for you, my friend, my lover.
A love that grows with each passing year,
Safe in the knowledge that you're always near.

I love you now and forever, I will,
Just as long as your arms I continue to fill.
Tell me you love me and be my Valentine,
'Cos there's no other man that I would want for mine.

THE ALTERNATIVE VALENTINE'S ODE
Written 20th January 1998 at Weight Management class.
Yes! I am still attending!

If you love me, don't buy me sweets,
Give me flowers or fat-free treats.
Bring me a cuppa without the sugar
Then I can stay your neater HUGGER!

Take me for a meal 'cos I love to dine,
Light the candle and say you'll be mine.
I can pick whatever The Diet will cover
And then I can stay your slimmer LOVER!!

MR CHAIRMAN, LADIES & GENTLEMEN
Written for and read at
Delamere 41 Club Ladies' Night - February 1997
with apologies to Lewis Carroll

The Time has come, Keith Wallace, Sir,
To talk of many things
Of cars and bikes and tractor tyres
Of a burglar alarm that rings.
And why a man slept in his loo
And whether cars have wings.

Some tales I will tell are known to many
And some are known to just a few
But by the time I'm finished with this little poem
We'll all be as wise as you.

T'was on a Burns Night, many years ago,
The Whisky had gone down well
Just how many bottles had been drunk
I doubt if anyone here could tell.

Drunk as lords, you all went back to the Bull,
Chains got lost and shoes were floated
You chauffeured Bryan home in his car
'Cos his head was tight and bladder bloated.

You returned him safely to his home
And left him in their downstairs loo.
You rang Sybil up the following day
Saying "I'll bring your car back to you".

You hadn't thought to let her know
That her husband was in the house
She found him exactly as you'd left him,
In the loo, asleep like a mouse.

Now picture the scene, it's a sunny day
And Moss Farm is agog with folk
It's called "It's a Knockout" for charity
And we all have a laugh and a joke

Volleyball with balloons full of water
Wet T-shirts, the best ever seen.
But then you went round in that Tractor Tyre
And boy, Keith, was your face ever green.

Then there was the night at the Rotary Dinner
When you and Penny were invited
To sit on the table as Philip's guests
But your hosts' wrath was soon incited.

Before the meal was served you set about
To sell, as many as you were able,
Book after book of Raffle Tickets
For Delamere Forest Round Table.

Another incident is brought to mind
You were driving the babysitter back.
Then returning home, you lost control
And the car went careering off track.

When you returned to the scene, the car had gone,
Cheese Hill was there, and the ditch.
The quarry manager was most perplexed.
Had the car grown the wings of a witch?

T'was found, at last, lying all forlorn
The hedge had rebounded and hid it
But it had all the makings of a mystery,
A car-jack, a UFO, or WHO-DID-IT?

Now some of these tales relate to cars,
But you have also been known to ride
Alternative transport, to the Tiger's Head,
And you left it parked outside.

You never thought that a thief would nick
Penny's bike, with its baby seat.
But they did and we can only assume
That you grovelled at Penny's feet!

Just be careful tonight when you go home,
Make sure that the alarm is not set.
Or the police will arrive and decline your drink
But your company fined might get.

This tribute is done and on behalf of your friends,
I wish you a wonderful time.
Enjoy yourself, dance and get drunk
And I hope you that enjoyed this rhyme.

LEGO ~ BORING? ~ NEVER!
Written during a rather long presentation by Lego®

LEGO construction builds the mind,
Model making - the best you'll find.
From toddler to teens, it suits them all.
Even Mums and Dads can have a ball.

DUPLO Play Train leads the way,
When toddlers get down to serious play,
And Toolo lets them bang and hammer.
"We want more", you'll hear them clamour.

Building trains and ships, even a town,
LEGO is the toy they won't put down.
Playing with Pirates, Ice Planet or Castle
Keeps the kids quiet without any hassle.

As they get older, they find LEGO Space.
You can see the interest on their face.
LEGO TECHNIC, working mechanics one can build.
Imagination is stirred and dreams fulfilled.

The names LEGO and DUPLO are registered trade marks
of the LEGO Group and are used here by special permission

STRESSFUL SUNDAY
Written on 31st October 1999

I've had one of those days, you know the sort.
Nowt went right, even the elements fought.
The rain started the minute the washing was out.
Then the hoover blew up, boy did I shout.
There was a flash of light so I switched it off.
I put the power back on then I gave a cough
As the thing gave out a cloud of dust.
Is it safe enough now, as the cleaning's a must?

With all this messing I'd forgotten the roast.
My organising skill's given up the ghost.
Today is Sunday, supposed to be for rest
And here am I so totally stressed.
Dinner gets cooked, the joint is just right,
Yorkshire's filled with gravy, lovely sight.
Oh bums, that's the doorbell, who can it be?
Who is knocking, who's calling on me?

I hate cold gravy 'cos it starts to congeal.
As I go to the door, more stress do I feel.
And there before me are eight little ghouls,
Their parents dressed up, looking real fools.
Their mothers had gone to a lot of trouble.
My stress is gone, no it didn't double.
I admire their outfits and give them some money.
My stress is all gone, life's as sweet as honey.

THE BATTLE OF THE BEEF
*Written Saturday 30th October 1999,
in the middle of the legal furore with France*

Well I did my bit for this sceptred isle today.
I bought only British, no French, no way.
A nice piece of beef, sadly not on the bone.
And I found in the shop that I was not alone.

Many shoppers were doing just the same
Playing the French at their own little game.
French Golden Delicious were not our choice.
I just wish the PM would hear our voice.

Be proud to be British, don't sell us out.
Listen to our farmers as they start to shout.
Fight for our rights not for Spanish anglers.
Keep Britain ours, don't let the EU strangle us.

The French don't like us and we don't like them,
"Entente Cordiale"... well, isn't that a gem.
Twinning of towns, what's that all about?
It just gives local councils a bit more clout.

And why have we got that blooming Chunnel,
It's a physical tie, they could march through the tunnel
To invade our island with their foreign ways.
Keep Britain ours and yes, the pound stays.

Listen to the people as they talk in the street,
Women will show you, we'll vote with our feet.
We'll stop buying French, we'll show the 'frogs'.
We'll try to stop Britain going to the dogs.

I'm proud to be British and I'm five foot five,
I'll measure imperial as long as I'm alive.
So, Mr Blair, just think what you're doing.
This could be a decision you'll end up rueing.

We'd give up so much if we joined with France,
It would be their tune we would be made to dance.
They would make the rules to suit their ends.
We've never have liked them, never been friends.

We bailed them out that day at Dunkerque.
They didn't even thank us, though we did all the work.
They want to rule us and to be our master.
It would be a future fraught with disaster.

So wake up, Tony, while we've got a chance.
Don't give our island to those in France.
If we need to hold hands with another nation,
The US would be better, in my estimation.

They're still playing games with the EU ruling.
Who do the French think that they are fooling?
Will we ever get any financial relief
From the French not eating good British Beef?

LUNCH WITH LYNE
*Written on Wednesday, 10th February 1999,
whilst waiting at the Dinorben Arms, Bodfari*

I didn't think it was too hard, to find the well-known inn
Take the main road, turn off, seemed quite easy~not for Lyne.
My friend is not so happy, when she is driving solo.
She goes to London on her own, and Glasgow, in her Polo.

But if there is a turn off, to a 'B' road not an 'A',
That is when my dear friend seems to go astray.
So I sat and waited patiently and sipped my second Coke,
Resolving, as I sat there, not to treat it as a joke.

'Cause I know she'll be worried and going round the bend.
I'm sorry I suggested it, I hope she's still my friend.
Finally she made it and we sat and had our meal.
She was rather flustered, I knew that's how she'd feel.

And then we decided that we <u>would</u> 'do lunch' again
But somewhere on an 'A' road, but didn't settle when
I'll leave the venue up to her, it'll be safer in the end.
I'll just look forward to it ~ lunch with Lyne, my friend.

FOOTBALL FANATIC
Written for and on behalf of Toffee

Aagh, go on now, just one more kick,
Then I'll show I'm grateful with a sloppy lick.
Another minute 'cause I love playing ball,
Then I promise I'll come when I hear you call.

Yes, I know you're tired and feeling beat,
But that's 'cause you've only got two feet.
I can run twice as fast, 'cause I've got four.
I've got lots of energy, so let's play some more.

Alright, I'm sorry, it's gone in the flowers.
Yes, I know that gardening takes hours and hours,
But, just fetch my ball for me, save my neck,
Then you'll get the blame if the blooms you wreck!

I can dribble the ball and nose it into the air,
I can pass it back to you with skill and flair.
You like to show off all my footballing tricks...
So, go on, just give me a few more kicks.

THE BLUE LINE
Written after my brush with breast cancer in 1992
I was bullied into this by my daughters.

I had this niggle at the back of my mind,
When I felt my breast, I knew what I'd find.
Yes, there was a lump, it didn't hurt at all;
But it took some time for me to make the call.

I made the appointment and went to see the Doc,
(That's Milroy ~ Patrick ~ he's up on the Rock).
I told him I'd several things bothering me,
My foot, my elbow, my ears ~ and he said, "Let's see".

Foot ~ trapped nerve ~ a cortisone injection.
Ears ~ not blocked but a catarrhal infection.
Elbow ~ as in Tennis ~ Sports Gel and rest.
Oh, by the way ~ I've a lump on my breast.

Examination over and I listened as he said,
"Halton ~ Mammogram", the words invaded my head.
"I'll write them a letter and you can collect it.
You can go when you like, your time ~ you select it."

A few weeks later I bared my chest
And between two 'plates' my boob was pressed.
She told me to wait while she looked at the 'pics',
And then she said, "I'll be back in two ticks."

"I'd like Dr Conway to have a look at these."
That was when I went weak at the knees.
She returned and said, "Tomorrow, if you can,
Please come back, we'll do an Ultra Scan."

I went for the Scan, they looked at the screen.
Dr Conway said, "There's two lumps to be seen.
You're going to need surgery. I'll fax your GP."
I think it frightened me, all the alacrity.

My bottle had gone, I felt in a muddle.
I rang my husband ~I needed a cuddle.
I knew what it was, the niggle now was real.
In a way I was relieved, what else could I feel?

An hour later, I was in the Doc's room.
He said, "I'm sorry to be a Prophet of Doom.
Ring this number, they'll do the rest.
See Mr H ~ the best in the North West."

At six o'clock, I made the call,
The appointment made, no trouble at all.
The following afternoon, Wednesday at 3.00,
Again the speed was worrying me.

I must admit, I didn't sleep too well.
What can you say and who can you tell?
My children were shocked, they all looked glum,
This couldn't happen, not to their Mum.

I got through the morning, it seemed so slow,
A coffee, a crossword, the time didn't go.
At last it was lunchtime, what to eat?
I'm ill, I thought, so I 'pigged out' a treat!

At half past one there was a knock at the door.
It was one of my neighbours, who'd lived <u>here</u> before.
I told her I was going to see her good friend,
She told me the routine and it helped no end.

She'd had both breasts done at the same place.
So I knew the procedure and what I'd to face.
She gave all the details and was very precise,
"The needle biopsy ~ it hurts and it's not very nice."

"But take it from me, you will be alright.
You'll be in hospital for only one night.
They treat you like royalty and feed you well,
And when you come out, no-one can tell."

"The scar is not massive, it's really quite neat,
And when wearing bikinis it's very discreet.
You'll be cut underarm, so that they can check."
It sounded quite simple, but I thought, "Oh Heck!"

What if they find it has spread around?
Inside I was screaming but there was no sound.
"Take it one day at a time," my friend said,
"Keep all the niggles and doubts out of your head."

So off I went, with my husband in tow,
I tried to be brave and not let the panic show.
Mr H was charming and talked so calm,
He examined my breast and under my arm.

He did the biopsy with a needle so thick,
He said, "I'm sorry, it won't be a 'little prick'."
He said it would hurt and he was quite right,
I gritted my teeth and clenched my fists tight.

Then two minutes later we were fixing 'the day'.
"I can't come next week, 'cause I'm going away.
I'll come after my hols, I'll need the rest."
He said "I'll let you know the results of the test."

He rang on the Friday and gave me the news,
"It is malignant, but don't get the blues.
We can take it all out with a minor op,
Don't worry, you won't be having the major chop."

I went on my holiday, Egypt was great,
I hardly thought of my awaiting fate.
Rameses, Nefertiti, Tutankhamun and the rest,
All the women on the tombs have only one breast!

The day arrived, my suitcase was shut,
I had a brown line for Mr H to cut.
I went to the hospital, arrived at eleven,
By half past one I was in 'pre-med' heaven.

At half past five I sat up for my tea,
A three-course meal especially for me.
My husband and daughters arrived at eight
And they stayed, watching telly, till really late.

The following day my dressings were changed,
My boob was still there, not re-arranged.
It was wrapped in 'cling-film', totally clear.
The nurse said "That's doing fine, my dear."

"We'll take the drip out after a while,
And then you go home." she said with a smile.
I was there for only about thirty hours
But my room was full of fruit and flowers.

My friend from Yorkshire had come to see me,
She didn't realise they were about to free me.
She drove me home, just in time for tea;
They were surprised to see her ~ followed by me!

My friend from Yorkshire had come to see me,
She didn't realise they were about to free me.
She drove me home, just in time for tea;
They were surprised to see her ~ followed by me!

I had a few days of being pampered,
But quickly felt my sanity hampered.
On the Thursday it was the General Election,
So I walked sedately and made my selection.

When I went out shopping, I found with glee
That people I met were surprised to see
That I was alive and kicking and looking well,
They thought I was dead, in heaven or hell!

They'd heard that I had been "seriously ill",
You know the fear that "Cancer" can instill.
Because I had been missing for quite a while,
They thought I'd 'gone' ~ it made me smile.

"A mild touch of Cancer" was what they heard,
I took sadistic joy in saying that word,
To see their faces and watch them pale,
Every time and every one, all without fail.

I hadn't felt ill, didn't look worse for wear.
I felt a sense of victory that I wanted to share.
Life is so precious, at least that much I learned,
It is a gift, but its quality must be earned.

After several weeks, Clatterbridge beckoned me,
I needed the "Planning" and had to see Dr E.
He put my boob into a kind of frame,
I'm sure if I had asked he'd have told me its name.

Measurements were taken and notes were written down.
We then went to Planning and he started to frown.
"Take a seat, there's a few waiting, nothing to fear.
I'll just pop inside and tell them you're here."

My name, at last, was called and I went inside,
Bared to the waist, to a bed I was 'tied'.
"Keep perfectly still, it won't take too long."
They make witty chat to jolly you along.

Out came the marker pens, thick and blue,
Followed the calibrations, straight and true.
My boob looked so silly, with all those crosses,
But they said, "That's fine." and they're the bosses.

Off I drive down the M Fifty Three,
A lovely May day, as hot as can be.
By the time I get home, the lines are smudged!
Next morning my sheets are totally fudged.

There's blue all over, except on my breast,
So I rang them up and 'got it off my chest'.
They said, "Don't worry, we can sort it out.
When you start your treatment, give us a shout."

My lines have now vanished, none to be seen,
There's only faint traces, where any have been.
"There's a queue for Planning, as long as can be.
Go have a coffee, maybe as many as three!!"

The Tea Bar is full of people and chatter,
Some are in uniform, for snacks and a natter.
Most of the faces look bright and cheery,
But there is the odd one that seems a bit weary.

Everyone here has a link with the next,
"Carcinoma" it's called in Dictionary text.
"Cancer" is the word that strikes hearts with fear ~
But that's outside ~ it is accepted in here.

My butties are eaten, my coffee is drunk,
I look down the corridor ~ no, the queue hasn't shrunk.
It's a hive of activity with patients and porters,
Ladies for therapy who've come with their daughters.

At last it's my turn, my name is shouted.
They can't believe their eyes, they really doubted.
No lines, no crosses, so what did they do?
They re-did them and threatened "Next time ~ Tattoo!"

Off down the corridor to M Five Three,
There's quite a few waiting as well as me.
I find myself looking for tell-tale blue lines,
We've all got them somewhere, the 'direction signs'.

As I sit and watch the people come and go
I think "It may be a killer, but it doesn't show."
All the people that I meet chat like an old chum,
It's not like a surgery where everyone's glum.

We sit and we listen to the X-Ray 'buzz',
You get used to the noise, everyone does.
I wait in the hallway until they are ready,
Then it's "Arms up and lie quite steady."

The machine starts up, the 'buzz' is mine,
Twenty-one seconds, and I'm feeling fine.
The nurses come back and they move the machine,
Then dash back out to watch on their screen.

Another twenty-one seconds and then a hush,
The nurses return, they're all in a rush.
"You can put your arms down now," they say,
"See you the same time, same place, next day."

I say, "Cheerio" and "See you tomorrow",
It's really a cheery place, no room for sorrow.
There's cards and flowers from 'Blue Liners' past.
For those who have been here, the memory will last.

One session down, twenty-three more to go.
They say it's not painful, those in the know.
"You may get a bit sick and maybe a bit tired,
And towards the end your boob will look 'fired'."

Each morning I worked till it was time to go,
Then off I set at a pace decidedly not slow.
It felt like escape as I put my foot down,
There was a smile on my face, no worried frown.

The staff they greet you with a smile and kind word,
And as you sit and wait, no moaning is heard.
The waiting room is light and bright and cheery,
And I'm greeted with "Nice to see you, deary."

A lady in her wheel-chair smiles at me,
She's got her blue lines all over her knee.
She's half way through her course of twenty,
As for good humour, she's got plenty.

And there's a man sitting there, lines on his head,
He's a real card, he tells me his name if Fred.
He's come by ambulance, travelling for hours,
Through country lanes, midst trees and flowers.

He goes in before me, they 'buzz' his brain.
"See you all tomorrow, I'll be back again."
There's no despondency, everyone's got hope,
That is what makes it much easier to cope.

Half way through my course, as I'm driving back,
I think, "My goodness, one of my boobs is black,
But it doesn't look damaged, apart from the colour,
In fact the other looks quite a bit duller."

So Radiotherapy is doing its best,
Burning the cancer out of my breast.
They had said at the start that it might not work,
But I set my mind positive ~ no doubts did lurk.

I did get tired but didn't feel sick,
Sucking a butterscotch soon did the trick.
I had my lunch then popped into town,
No way was Cancer going to get me down.

Every day I would have a half hours' sleep,
That's a luxury that I wish I could keep!
Then up in time to cook the dinner -
Between me and cancer, I was the winner.

Now the time has passed and my scar has healed,
I've even sunned topless (in a far off field).
But I'm back in the rat-race, working like mad -
My 'Blue Line' days were the healthiest I've had!

My check-ups show that there's no cause to worry,
The Cancer's not coming back, well not in a hurry.
My thanks to all the wonderful medical team,
You made this woman's nightmare seem like a dream!

LADIES OF M~5~3
Written to thank the nurses at Clatterbridge

It has been a joy to know you,
        the team on the M~5~3
This poem is just to show you
        I'm as grateful as can be.
You treat us all so kindly
        all the ladies and the men,
As we lie there oh so blindly
        when you wield that little blue pen
Those blue felt lines went crazy,
        they're on bras and on the sheet.
And if they went a little hazy
        you did them again ~ so neat.
Now my treatment's nearly done,
        no more "Hands on head" or "Still".
The lines will fade but not in the sun.
        But my memories of you never will.

THANKS TO THE POCKET ROCKET
Written for Fran Potts on 1st April 1999
- her Charity Night for Breakthrough

I am here, tonight, to thank you, Fran
My friend that I call 'Pocket Rocket'
And also every woman and man
Who've put their hand in their pocket.

Fran and I have both had the chop
We've both felt the surgeon's knife
But neither of us worried about the op
And neither feared for our life.

This disease we've had claims rather a lot
One in twelve is the hit rate today.
Three hundred a week, they recover not.
So we've been rather lucky, I'd say.

It is frightening the toll that it takes
Fourteen hundred a month is the sum
But positive thinking the difference makes
When you don't let it make you glum.

The money that you're raising tonight
Is going to a fighting cause.
To find a cure, to make it right
So it doesn't claim you or yours.

On behalf of Breakthrough, I thank you all
The amount Fran makes is real wealth.
And, as for myself, I've had a ball
So thank you, Fran, Good Luck and Good Health.

A SPECIAL DAY
Written on the train back from London,
Wednesday 8th December 1999

I went to meet a Prince today and hoped to shake his hand.
This is the man who will, one day, be King of this fair land.
He arrived with sirens blaring, bodyguards all around
And when he came into the room some space for him was found.

We stood in hope, like sardines pressed, to get a closer look
But every time my camera aimed, behind someone he'd duck!
His guards moved oh so slowly, clearing out his way.
Oh would we get to meet him, t'would make our special day.

And then he's gone right past us, we didn't catch his eye,
That's Judith James [North Wales], Liz [Merseyside] and I.
We went into a huddle and we came up with a plan.
We'd 'cut him off at the pass', like Mounties we'd get our man!

He is the Patron of our Charity ~ 'Breakthrough' ~ that's its name.
To find a cure for Breast Cancer, that's its hope and all our aim.
We three are just a small few of the many who were there
To see the Centre opened by Prince Charles, the Monarch's heir.

We moved towards the exit and waited patiently.
There was no way we'd be ignored, the eager Northern three.
Oh! Drat! He's got his back to us, he's heading for the door!
In just a sec he'll get away and be gone for ever more!

And then Liz collared Delyth, "What about Merseyside?"
She turned the Prince of Wales around, we shook his hand
                                              with pride.
But someone went one better, she beat us by lots and lots.
My Pocket Rocket got a hug from him, yes, I mean Fran Potts!

"AMAZING MISS JONES"
Written after a visit to Sandiway Manor - 22 July 1998

Today I met the lady who inspired this little ode.
She resides in Sandiway Manor, a magnificent abode.
Her hair is white, her face and her body wrinkled,
But when she shook my hand, her eyes they really twinkled.

I went to visit, with my friend, to borrow from their china.
As a retirement home, I have not seen one finer.
The job complete, crockery safely loaded in the car,
We went to see some ladies and ask them how they are.

Then we went up stately stairs, with panelling so fine.
(No-one ever mounts these stairs going up two-at-a-time.)
Along to the end of the corridor and then a gentle knock.
Then in we go, my friend and I, and then I get a shock.

Here is this amazing lady, with eyes bright as a bird.
And as for years of age, she is in her ninety-third.
She wants to go out shopping - my friend will drive her there.
She knows just where she wants to go, not just anywhere!

I hope with all my heart, when old age comes my way,
Somewhere like Sandiway Manor is where I spend my day.
And when my face is wrinkled and I ache in all my bones,
I hope I will age with dignity, like you have, dear Miss Jones.

THE BALLADING BUTCHER
*Written about Tony who worked
in the local butcher's shop*

He sings while he's working,
So bright and so cheerful.
He's never seen shirking,
And we all get an earful.
He never just sings the same old ballad,
He's always 'changing his tune'.
The songs are as varied as any fruit salad.
He'll sing some rock or maybe just croon.
You stand in the queue, your order in hand;
You wait and you listen to Tone.
Now it's your turn and your mind goes bland,
Was it beef, pork or ham-on-the-bone?
No-one's offended when he sings out loud,
It keeps us all cheerful and bright.
Saturday mornings, there's always a crowd,
Some just wonder - does he practice at night?
Keep up the singing, with cleaver in hand,
Let nothing discourage that beat.
Just ask your customers - that happy band,
Do we come for the songs or the meat?

A FEW THAT HAVE BEEN 'COMMISSIONED'

MARRIAGE LINES
Written for wedding stationery customers

Dianne is a pretty young nurse,
Andrew you see for a curse -
No - Swearing an Oath!
Good Luck to you both,
From the Printer who thought up this verse.

Your instructions were precise and exact,
Are you like that when you're at Rotoract?
I'm glad that you typed out the Manx -
It saved me some worries - so Thanks!

I hope this ASSIGNMENT you've planned,
With happiness will go hand in hand.
I hope the OPERATION is a success,
Best Wishes, Good Luck and God Bless.

THE DOG HOUSE
Written for Angie

If your dog is looking tatty
And he's got lumps of matted hair,
If he's looking decidedly ratty,
Get him groomed, it's only fair.

Your dog will feel much better
When he's been bathed and clipped.
And then 'blown dry', if he'll let her
And between his claws are clipped.

The Dog House is the place to go,
He deserves it, your much-loved pet.
Angie will make him fit to show.
A better grooming he could not get.

The place may look slightly altered,
The decor has been re-arranged.
But Angie's grooming has not faltered,
Only the name on the cards has changed.

~~~~~~~~~

When you bring your dog in for a groom,
Look around, we have no spare room.
So when you know the clipping's over
Please collect your 'Lady', 'Spot' or 'Rover'.
If doggy collection is long delayed
A charge of £5 per hour will be made.
We love your dogs and they love us
But they should go home and have a fuss.

MERRY CHRISTMAS SIR
Written 10th December 1999
for the Head of Huntingdon School

Lurking in the Santa's Grotto was a boy called John,
Standing waiting for his gift, with new trousers on.
He also wore a new shirt with creases not a hint,
Hair was slicked down and breath as fresh as mint.
He opened up his present. He stood there and he roared,
"This is just what I asked for, chalk, ruler and blackboard."

ENGAGING WORDS

Written to celebrate Christian and Carolann's engagement

We couldn't find a card that wasn't
    twee and sloppy,
We thought that if we sent you one,
    you'd get a little stroppy.
We wanted to send "Congratulations"
    to a very special mate.
We'll save the "bows and ribbons"
    till you've gone and set
        THE DATE!

MOVING HOME
Written for Rev and Mrs Robinson, Saughall

I hope you'll be happy in your new abode,
With old friends around you, just down the road.
It is time to take it easy, sit down and have a rest,
You've given of yourselves and you've done your best.
The shackles are off after thirty seven years -
Good Health, Long Life, God Bless, my dears.

~~~~~~~~~~~~~~~~~~~~

MOVING TIMES
Written 26th November 1999
to John, Sylvia and family when they left Alvanley

We hope that you'll be happy
        in your new home, far away.
We knew the move was coming
        ~ shame you couldn't stay.
You'll all be missed in Alvanley,
        especially at the school.
[I heard from Chris, the secretary,
        they've dried the teary pool.]
You became much more than 'tenants'
        ~ that's what we like to think,
If ever you are passing by,
        please stop and have a drink.
And don't forget, on Bonfire Night,
        when the sky is full of sparks,
We'll send a rocket southwards,
        especially for the Clarkes.

THE DOCTOR'S WAITING ROOM
Written 13th July 1999

'Phones are ringing, patients waiting,
Who'll be next they're all debating.
The queue is growing, no call as yet.
A lady needs the bus, starts to fret.

Across the room there is no queue.
A patient comes, appointment due.
Within two tics her name is heard.
Is her doctor to be preferred?

We sit and wait, hearing voices.
The tannoy making no more noises.
Seven minutes is what you get
When into the room you are let.

At last, a name, the queue moves on.
More than seven minutes have gone.
Then another, it's not too bad.
It's my turn next, I am so glad.

Then my name and in I go.
Is there a stop-watch there on show?
I take my seat, the telephone rings.
This will delay the speed of things.

Then he's done, it was his wife,
And now I pour out all my strife.
IBS, weight loss, and passing out.
"It's stress - there is a lot about."
continued.......

"Take these tablets when they're needed."
Instructions that I've always heeded.
"If I could find a cure for stress,
I'd be a millionaire, no less."

The Doctor is always running late
And I had worried about the wait.
My stress is something that I hoard
But he takes everyone's on board.

Maybe I should learn to 'chill'
And then I wouldn't feel so ill.
Patience is a virtue, so it's said,
Better be patient than end up dead!

EDUCATION'S A WONDERFUL THING

EXAM NERVES
Sent to my daughter, Sarah, during her University days

Water Resources Technology -
        that's S..T to you and me!
Chemistry - was it really as bad
        as you thought that it would be?
Carbon Monoxide, VOCs,
        Nitrogen Dioxide, et al,
These will all fly out of your pen,
        and then it's done, my gal.
I don't know what the subject is
        of the one you've got today,
But by this time next week you'll be
        watching Wimbledon each day!

THE JOYS OF TEACHING?
Sent to my daughter, Anne-Louise, during her teaching practice

When all your woes surround you,
And you're feeling down in the dumps,
And the class just doesn't work fast enough,
And your path seems full of 'humps';
Think of the worst thing that could happen....
Every child could become an 'Annie-Lou'!
Then you really would have problems,
With thirty-odd 8 year-old versions of YOU!

JAMES' FIRST
Sent to him on hearing that he had got a First

Well done, congrats, on getting a First,
I bet you heart was ready to burst.
The day will come when you go back to 'Kings'
And face the doubters - stupid things!

You've proved them wrong and in good style.
You've proved the hard work was all worthwhile.
Your Olympic efforts have gained you a Gold.
Good Luck for the future, whatever it may hold.

BLAIR'S BABY
Written after reading that Cherie Blair [45]
is expecting a baby in May 2000

Well am I surprised, no, not one little bit.
'Politically planned pregnancy' is what I thought of it.
A babe for the Millennium, and in middle age,
Gets the Prime Minister more of front page.

I can't help feeling that it was totally planned
To try and give Tony the upper hand.
There they will be with a babe in their arms
Electioneering with all their charms.

Conceived, so we're told, in Tuscany,
Created European in central Italy.
Middle-aged Mum is what Cherie Blair will be
Not Mrs PM or Mrs Blair QC.

Political one-up-manship, what a coup.
It may gain some votes, I hope only a few.
I just hope they realise it's a baby's life
And a serious risk for the PM's wife.

Baby Leo was born 20th May 2000

CHRISTMAS IN VERSE
Written one Christmas when time and rhyme were plenty!

Rob, I hope you'll find your 'niche' one day
In a job that will give you time to play.
Have a Merry Christmas with all your friends
And I hope your happiness never ends.

~~~~~~~~~~

To my daughter, Sarah, this I wish,
May the New Year find you a hunky dish!
I hope your Christmas will be a ball
With presents galore from one and all.

~~~~~~~~~~

Anne-Louise, my daughter dear,
May your Christmas time be full of cheer.
May the New Year bring a lot of fun
But only when all your work is done.

~~~~~~~~~~

We hope your Christmas will be bright and merry,
With plenty of beer, lager, wine or sherry.
E.J. we hope you will enjoy your break
And in the New Year, the new headship will take.
Chris, we wish you life with a bit more ease,
With time out of the office to do as you please.
And all the best, Carl, in your final year.
And so, Merry Christmas and Happy New Year.

continued.......

CHRISTMAS IN VERSE
continued

May your Christmas, Mum, be a bright time,
With family and friends calling in.
And we will be there Boxing Night time,
To join in the family din.

May your pipe, Dad, always be well packed,
May your garden always look neat,
And may the shelves in the shed be well stacked
For when you want to go and put up your feet.

A very Merry Christmas with plenty of cheer,
With presents to open, all things new.
Good Health is wished for the New Year
From both of us to both of you.

~~~~~~~~~~~~~~~~~~~~~

Will Benjamin get more for his Game Gear,
And be 'plugged in' like he was last year?
Will Olivia take up the stage for a living?
Will Janet stir more people into giving?
And will Barry get round 'under par'
And celebrate by buying a car?
Whatever you all wish for the New Year
Is wished by all those who signed here.

SUMMERS, PAST AND PRESENT
Written August 1997

These hot summer days are quite a pleasure,
They remind me of the 60s, memories I treasure.
The long school holidays, Augusts long past,
When the glorious sunshine seemed to last and last.

I would ride my Vespa with the screen removed.
(Still quite safe, but my mum disapproved.)
The threat of skin cancer was never around
And I went back to school all nicely browned.

Now the sun beats down and I don't want to work,
When it is really hot, I would rather shirk.
I envy the schoolkids with their lazy days...
Even my dog has got sun-bathing ways!

The best I will get is an al fresco meal,
But the sun's still warm, the heat I can feel.
So it's on with a sun-top and off with my tights.
I cope with the days, but those summer nights!!

THE DAY I DIED
*Written on the Anniversary of my visit to
Leeds Royal Infirmary - November 1952*

I want to tell you a story........about the day I died.
The images are, oh so clear, I cherish them inside.
If I was an artist I could paint for you the scene.
I remember telling people I had seen the Fairy Queen.

My heart had a hole in it, which really needed closing.
The task before the surgeon, I'm told, was rather quite
                                                              imposing.
The odds of fifty-fifty were what my folks were told.
The op had never been done before on a child just six
                                                              years old.

"A matter of life or death," they heard, " there really is no
                                                              choice."
And so they gave permission, both with solemn voice.
My parents said I was in theatre for over eight long hours,
But all I can remember is the colour of all those flowers.

I walked towards the bright light, flowers all around.
Every single colour was there, bursting from the ground.
I can't remember turning back, but obviously I did,
But the images are crystal clear, though I was just a kid.

SLIMMERS PLEA
Written at Slimming Club, January 1997, as self-motivation!!!

I think I'm fat, no ~I **KNOW** I'm fat,
A look in the mirror reminds me of that!
I'm a chocoholic and, yes, I like a drink,
But I **COULD** lose weight if I stop and think!
A conscious effort now and every day
Then my 'love-handles' might go away.
I **KNOW** I can do it, I **MUST** persevere,
But I **DO** need help, that's why I'm here!

TO ABSENT FRIENDS AND LOVED ONES

MY DAD
Written over a long period of time

Oh, my goodness, I do miss my Dad.
He was the best friend that I ever had.
Don't get me wrong, I do miss my Mum,
But she was my mother and not like a chum.

Under his arm I could shelter from harm,
He was a giant, but gentle and calm.
He could nod off in seconds and snore like a bear,
I would tease him about it but he didn't care.

He was 'built for comfort and not for speed',
Of high fashion trends he took no heed.
His trilby for best and flat cap for work,
No other hats in wardrobe did lurk.

He rode his bike with one leg at an angle,
So that the basket of eggs he could dangle.
An ordinary bike was never quite right,
But one 'plus a bit' gave him extra height.

He didn't swear often, but once, when drunk,
He came home smelling worse than a skunk.
In the chicken run he had fallen full length,
He needed deodorant but triple the strength!

His language was colourful, as strong as the smell.
He told 'the old battle axe' to 'go to Hell'!
Grandma was stunned, but she didn't get mad,
She just walked backwards, away from my Dad.

For a game of Whist, he would go to the Club,
BRSA - the railway mens' pub.
He played in the league, won many a cup.
When they played away, boy, did they sup.

They would go off early - they went by bus.
Why not train, was it too much fuss?
They would stop at every pub on the way
Determined to enjoy the whole of the day.

Sometimes he would come back really late.
I would hear him fighting the garden gate.
He would creep upstairs, well he thought he crept,
Trying not to disturb my Mum as she slept.

Grunting and groaning as he got undressed,
Any swearing was being well suppressed.
Then I would hear the creaking bed
Next the noise as he started to Zed

Like a lumberjack's saw, the snoring sound,
Quite the loudest of the noises around.
He slept through the racket like a little kid.
He slept OK, but no-one else did.

I once taped the noise, as he slept in the chair.
'Z-Cars' was on, but he didn't care.
I turned down the telly and pressed 'record',
And, unaware, he laid there and snored.

Once, as he slept, I covered his face
With dots of Nivea, all over the place.
And then he stirred from his noisy sleep.
I ran and hid, my secret to keep.
continued..........

He rubbed his face, with a startled look,
The cream went in every wrinkle and nook.
"I didn't feel a single thing" he said,
"I sleep so deep, I could be dead."

When we went walking I would always ride,
High on his shoulders, not by his side.
As I grew older I'd try to match his pace.
But he walked so fast as if in a race.

I remember the day, my driving test passed,
I gave him a lift - the first and the last.
He sat on the pillion, I started to frown.
I just couldn't hold the front wheel down!

The day I got married, he swelled with pride
To have his young daughter walk by his side.
As he gave his speech, with a tear in his eye,
I wanted to hug him and I wanted to cry.

He loved the children, didn't see them for long.
He was taken away, it seemed so wrong.
He was Rob's best mate, they gardened all day.
He was always ready when Rob wanted to play.

The girls weren't quite two when he took his leave.
It still really hurts and I just cannot believe
That a giant so gentle, so kind and so fair,
When I really need him, he just isn't there.

TO MY MUM
Written over a period of time

My Mum was the eldest of a family of five.
None of them, sadly, are still alive.
She was the only girl, with brothers four.
She ruled the roost and gave them what for.

She had lots of boyfriends, from their mates,
But they always followed when she went on dates.
If they saw her kissing, they went and told Gran.
Mum would get mad - oh, how they ran!

When they got married it was Boxing Day.
This was Dad's choice, she would always say.
Then no-one could see him getting wed.
Only the family saw Lorna marry Ted.

When she got older, she was always ill.
She coughed herself red, I can hear her still.
She never recovered from losing my brother,
It was so unfair, what happened to Mother.

She worked so hard, to make ends meet.
Some days she was almost dead on her feet.
She fretted like mad when Dad was late.
Dashed to greet him at the garden gate.

She taught me to crochet, sew and knit.
Though knitting gave her a coughing fit.
When I was small she made my dresses.
And as I grew up she permed my tresses.

continued...........

She would have a day to bake and bake,
Buns and tarts and chocolate cake.
Date and Walnut and Currant bread,
And custard tarts just for Ted.

Her fluffy sponges were second to none,
It didn't take long before they were all gone.
She couldn't make bread, her 'hand' was too light,
But for making those sponges it was just right.

She loved my children and spoiled them rotten.
I just hope all her love will not be forgotten.
Crunchies on Fridays, their weekly treat.
After school they would run down the street.

That she was taken so soon, seems unfair.
When the children grew up she wasn't there.
She would have been proud of them getting on.
I tell her these things, even though she has gone.

TO THE QUEEN OF HEARTS
Written for, and read at, my Auntie Mabel's funeral

So much of my life has memories of you
That a poem in your honour was the least I could do.
Closer than my real aunts, you were my Aunt Mabel,
So I'll recall a few tales, in verse, if I'm able.

I remember one day, it was Nineteen Fifty Three,
It really was a very special day for me.
I sat on the sofa with Sandy on my lap,
Despite the occasion, she still had her nap.

We all sat there and gazed in awe,
The Queen's Coronation was what we saw.
The grandest thing I had ever seen,
And all displayed on a twelve inch screen.

Dad and I used to come on the train,
Having left Mum shopping in town, again.
We would watch TV, then have some tea,
Then play Newmarket, the bet ~ one old P.

When it was time, old Bunty would know,
She would look for her lead so she could go.
A walk to the station, at dead of night,
Uncle Bill took a torch to give us light.

Then on Summer Sundays, we'd go for a ride
And take a trip to the countryside.
I sat in the back of the van, heard but not seen,
The places I saw were where we had been!

continued.......

David and Peter came for supper, with mates.
And then, years later, it was with their dates.
Midnight would strike, it was Christmas Day,
Presents were opened, then you were on your way.

Boxing Days to Laxton for a super spread,
And cheating at cards, 'twas either Bill or Ted.
Someone would make the Jack of Clubs hide.
(I still have Mum's tin with the pennies inside.)

I remember the race between Wyvern and Van,
David and Peter (he was going out with Ann).
They raced down the lanes with speed and flair
Then into the yard with inches to spare.

The pigs, I recall, were all pink and clean,
David had those (he was going out with Jean).
The hens and chicks, the fruit and the veg,
And nice friendly neighbours looking over your hedge.

I remember your scones and tea from spotted cups,
And watching Bunty with her phantom pups.
To my Mum you were more like sisters than cousins
And, as Auntie Mabel, you've left memories in dozens.

Christmas Eve was always a great event,
Dying to know what presents were sent.
You and Uncle Bill would come over for tea.
Newmarket was played for an hour or three.

All these memories, and so many more,
My mind seems to hold an endless store.
Each tale I recall seems touched with gold
And all become brighter when they are told.

As I say my farewell, I know, with God's will
That you will be re-united with Uncle Bill.
My life is full of memories of you, Auntie Mabel,
Especially when my cards are out on the table.

FAREWELL TO NORA
Written for the funeral service of my Mother-in-Law
December 1996

We are all here today to say our last farewell
To Nora, a lady who fitted that word so well.
We come as a loved one, as family or as a friend,
To say "Goodbye", but it isn't really the end.
Each has a memory that can be held in the heart
Because in all our lives she played her part,
As Wife, as Mother, Grandma and Sister too;
As Auntie, as Friend, as Neighbour to you.
Hold on to the memory, please don't let it fade ~
It will ease the sorrow that her parting has made.

ONE OF A KIND
Written on the death of our friend, Stan

He was one of a kind, for sure, dear Stan.
They broke the mould when they made that man.
He was life and soul of every meeting,
With jokes and tales and friendly greeting.
He leaves a space that will never be filled;
There are lots of memories that can't be killed.
We share the sorrow that his parting has made,
Knowing that those memories will never fade.

THE THIEF CALLED DEATH
Sent to a friend after the tragic death of her and Stan's young son

We couldn't make a 'phone call
    'cos our brains went out of gears,
At your tragic loss, so sudden,
    of one of tender years.
We tried to write a letter,
    but the words just were not there,
But our thoughts, they never left you,
    as your grief we share.
If there is any way at all,
    in which we can assist,
No matter what the task is,
    just add us to your list.
If you feel like ringing us,
    just to ask the question "Why?"
We will not have an answer,
    but as friends we sure would try.
We send our deepest sympathies
    to you all, the ones bereft,
And hope that time will heal,
    with the memories that are left.

THE THIEF CALLED DEATH REVISITS
Sent to a friend after the tragic death of George, her new-born son

I couldn't make a 'phone call,
    no words would bring you joy,
After your tragic loss, so sadly,
    of your little baby boy.
I tried to write a letter, but the words
    they just weren't there,
But my thoughts, they never left you,
    as your grief I tried to share.
If you feel like ringing me,
    just to ask the question "Why?"
I will not have an answer,
    but as a friend I sure would try.
I send my deepest sympathies
    to you all, the ones bereft,
And hope that time will heal,
    with the memories that are left.

see next page

A BUNDLE OF JOY, A LITTLE BOY
Written 20th April 2000 to celebrate the birth of Jack

Congratulations on the birth of your child.
I imagine the mood is deliriously wild.
At last you've got your bundle of joy,
And now you can hold your little boy.

To have this child you've gone through hell.
I'm really pleased it's worked out so well.
Memories of George'll come flooding back,
So you've got twice the love to give to Jack.

I'm sure Jack'll be the light of your lives,
George, in your hearts, still survives.
Jack, your son, is your dream come true.
I wish health and happiness to all of you.

GEORGIO THE GUIDE
Given to our holiday guide in Venezuela

Georgio, we will miss you after you have gone.
Your organisation for us was second to none.
From Caracas to Merida and Cuidad Bolivar,
You looked after us well, whether near or far.
You told us things travelling along in the bus
(Which arrived on time without any fuss.)
With your future crowds, we wish you well,
Adios amigo, it has been really swell.

"COLIN'S BOTTLE"
Written after his op, 3rd July 1998

"Will Grandpa have a 'bottle' at the end of his left leg?"
A three-and-a-half year old's image of a prosthesis with its peg.
"Better to have no foot, than a poorly one", said Mia.
Two little girls giving advice to one they love so dear.

And now we hear you're mobile, albeit in a chair,
It seems a long, long time since first you went in there.
When we came to visit, we didn't know what we'd find.
But then we heard <u>that</u> laugh of the very dirtiest kind!

You looked so hale and hearty, apart from the obvious bit.
And it soon was quite apparent you hadn't lost your wit.
We hope that all goes smoothly and you will soon be out.
Just behave in the meantime, don't make the nurses shout.

Now the op is over, your recovery should be speedy.
Don't hog that bed much longer, that is being greedy.
We know you love the attention, of nurses - short or tall.
Just get better quickly, lots of love from one and all.

GET WELL SOON
Written to Olga after she'd had her operation

Now that you're home but can't lift or drive,
Leave all the heavy stuff to Jonno or Clive.
If you want attention ~ just ring their bell.
Don't worry about housework ~ it can go to hell.

Your health is important, so don't decry it,
Needing to Hoover? Well, just don't try it.
Don't rush to be 'doing' or you may rue it.
Whatever it is ~ if it hurts ~ don't do it!

PROGRESS - A WONDROUS THING?
Written after trying to speak to Manweb, 17th Sept1997

I have just lost a morning, well it feels like that.
My brain has gone numb and my ear is quite flat,
Listening to "Greensleeves" and pressing 'the star'.
What sort of morons do these folk think we are?

I have dialled the right number, an 0 three, four, five,
But I would love to hear the voice of someone alive.
I've pressed the star button till my finger is numb,
By the time a human answers I've gone quite dumb.

It's the same when I ring the Bank, just ten miles away.
"Can I help you?" the man in Hemel Hempstead will say!
Where is it all going, this so-called HI-TECH?
All this impersonal service is a pain in the neck!

What happened to personal service, the human voice?
Now it's all computerised and we have no choice.
How much money do these companies really save?
I bet A.G. Bell is turning round in his grave!

AN INSOMNIAC'S DREAM
Written 12th January 2000
started at 3.00 am completed at 2.30 pm

They say it's a habit, this sleeping lark,
It's one I crave when I wake in the dark.
I go to sleep, with no trouble at all,
Then I'm awake, alert, on the ball.

It doesn't matter if I've had a drink or two,
Sleep still avoids me when drink's taboo.
I've tried swapping beds, reading my book,
Turning my pillow, sleeping ~ no luck.

It doesn't seem to matter what I try,
By two in the morning awake I lie.
Thoughts crowd my mind, I cannot sleep.
Some nights I just lay in my bed and weep.

"To sleep, perchance to dream" said the Bard,
It's the staying asleep that I find so hard.
I'd love to wake up feeling nice and bright.
I don't 'cos I've been awake half the night.

"Bright eyed and bushy tailed', what a laugh.
I wake up, most mornings, feeling totally naff.
I feel as though my body is taut, been 'wired'
And yet, here's the weird thing, I don't feel tired.

By the time breakfast's over I'm ready to work.
No thoughts about sleep in my mind do lurk.
By lunchtime my day is steadily plodding
But, what's this, oh dear, my head, it is nodding.

continued......

Dare I shut my eyes and have a snooze?
Then later there'll be no need for booze.
If I do sleep now, what about night time.
But my body's saying NOW is the right time.

NIGHTMARE
Written at 2.30 am whilst still shaking

Am I alone when I'm dreaming?
Why do I shout in my sleep?
Why do I wake sometimes, screaming?
What is it that makes my skin creep?

What is it that sets my pulse racing?
What scares me out of my skin?
Is it the Devil that I'm facing?
If so ~ what is he trying to win?

My astral relations total seven,
Each one a loved one and friend.
I've walked in the Garden of Eden,
I've seen the bright light at the end.

So don't try to frighten and scare me,
I know you're the dark side, you're sin.
But I'll take you on ~ if you dare me
'Cos I know that you'll never win!

MARKET MOTORING MADNESS
Written Thursday, 12th February 1998 at lunch-time

I've just done something I don't often do,
And I'm sure more people feel the same way too.
I drove through Frodsham Market ~ well, I tried...
Through the bit of road with vans at each side.
There were people trying to cross the street,
Stood in the middle, faces lined with defeat.
Van reversing, no parking to be had.
It's just a little crazy and it drives me mad.

But, I could have picked a much worse hour,
Ten to four is when it wields its power.
Traffic doubles, buses try to turn in vain,
But by now the road is down to one lane.
The traders are going, packing up their wares,
They park over their line and no-body cares.
Every direction but UP traffic seems to go,
Driving in Frodsham on Thursdays? Just say NO!

THE SCREAMING TREES
Written 10th April 2000 after hearing the tale

I heard a tale about some trees,
        it really was amusing.
I must admit though, parts of it
        were truly quite confusing.
The chainsaw roared, the woman screamed,
        the air was blue with cursing.
She claimed the trees were crying
        and they really would need nursing.
She called the men all sorts of things
        and then she called the law.
She claimed that she'd been threatened
        by Richard, with chainsaw.
They really were Paul's tree tops,
        they weren't even hers to save.
Yet all the local people heard
        the woman rant and rave.
She said she'd call the papers
        and tell her tale of woe
But Paul and Richard still agree,
        the trees have got to go.

ELEVEN O'CLOCK - 1 ACROSS
Written one morning at coffee time

Eleven o'clock, it's time for coffee.
Penguin for me, Rich Tea for Toffee.
Daily Telegraph and pen are ready.
No need to rush, just take it steady.

The clues are there in black and white,
Under two minutes to get it right.
Quick Crossword now, Cryptic later,
'Short and Snappy' - that's Alligator.

Two to go - a word for 'Blazing'
One to go with no erasing.
I do enjoy this mental test,
Best time yet ~ now I can rest.

The Quick one's done in one minute fifty.
If I say so myself t'was pretty nifty.
Now back to work 'til it's time for lunch
Then over the Cryptic I can hunch!